# At Night

*Margaret Peot*

For Mark

we jump in puddles

MuddyBootsBooks.com

An imprint of Globe Pequot, the trade division of
The Rowman & Littlefield Publishing Group, Inc.
4501 Forbes Blvd., Ste. 200
Lanham, MD 20706
www.rowman.com

Distributed by NATIONAL BOOK NETWORK

British Library Cataloguing in Publication Information available

Library of Congress Cataloging-in-Publication Data available

ISBN 978-1-4930-6184-6 (hardcover: alk. paper)
ISBN 978-1-4930-6364-2 (e-book)

Printed in Mumbai, India, June 2021

At night

owls hoot,

foxes play,

and bobcats watch
from the shadows.

At night

opossums dangle,

raccoons splash,

and rabbits hide
in the tall grass.

At night

skunks sniff,

mice forage,

and porcupines waddle

when it's time

. . . to sleep.

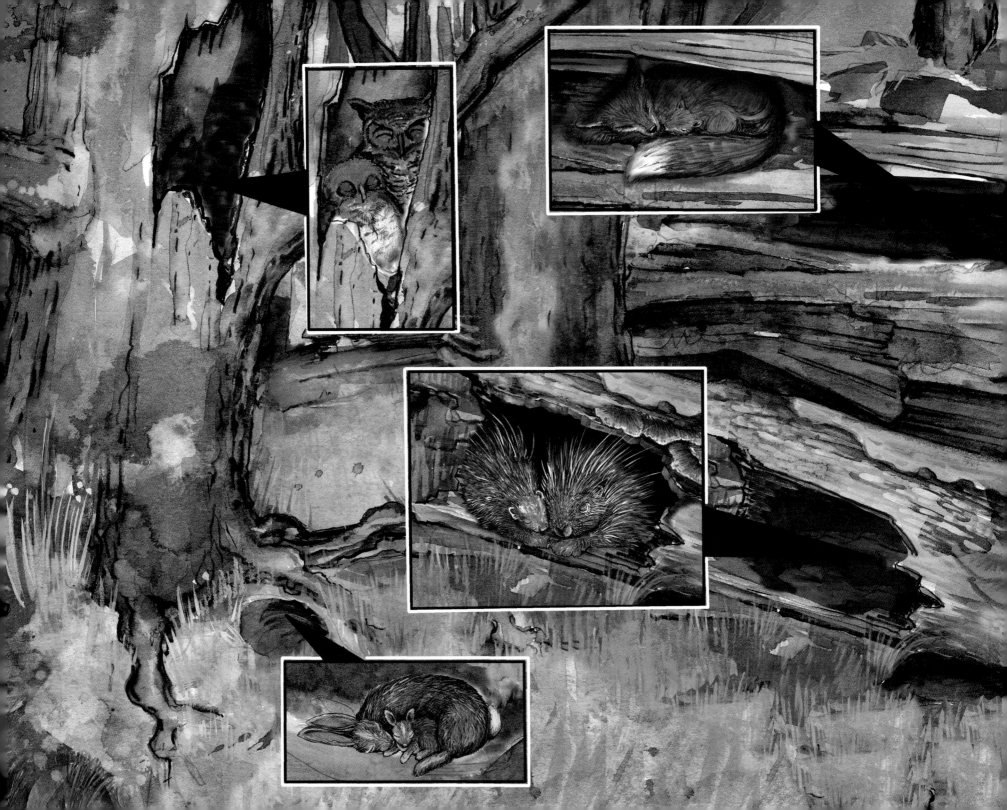

A baby fox is called a kit, and a group of foxes is called a skulk.

A baby porcupine is called a porcupette, and a group of porcupines is called a prickle.

A baby raccoon is called a kit or cub, and a group of raccoons is called a gaze.

A baby skunk is called a kit, and a group of skunks is called a surfeit.

A baby owl is called an owlet, and a group of owls is called a parliament.

A baby bobcat is called a kitten, and a group of bobcats is called a clowder.

A baby rabbit is called a kitten, and a group of rabbits is called a colony.

A baby opossum is called a joey, and a group of opossums is called a passel.

A baby mouse is called a pup, and a group of mice is called a mischief.

## About the Author

Margaret Peot is an artist, writer, and teacher, and she paints costumes for Broadway theater as well as for dance, ice, and arena shows. She is the author/artist of twelve other books, including *Inkblot: Drip, Splat, and Squish Your Way to Creativity*, which was awarded the Eureka! Silver Medal for nonfiction children's books. She lives in New York City.